Poetry is Our Ministry

"to Touch the Heart"

By: Anelda L. Ballard

Co-author Jean A. Scott

"Second Edition"

Poetry is Our Ministry "to Touch the Heart" *"Second Edition"*

By: Anelda L. Ballard

Co-author: Jean A. Scott

Cover Illustrated by: Jean A. Scott

Cover designed by: Elaine Lanmon

Logo designed by: Andre Saunders

Photography by: John "Rolex" Kollock of Philadelphia, PA,

www.photobucket.com and www.fotosearch.com

Hair Stylist: Tiffany of Newark, DE

Hair Stylist for Photo on Back Cover: Roxanne Meade

© 2005 Anelda L. Ballard

ISBN# 978-0-9768540-0-5

ISBN# 0-9768540-0-7

All rights reserved. This book is protected under the copyright laws of the United States of America. This book may not be copied or reprinted for commercial gain or profit. The use of short quotations or occasional page copying for personal or group study is permitted and encouraged. Permission will be granted upon request.

Scripture quotations are taken from the Maxwell Leadership Bible, King James Version, New King James Version, New International Version and the New Living Translation of the Holy Bible.

For Worldwide Distribution, Printed in the United States of America

Published by Jazzy Kitty Greetings Marketing & Publishing, LLC

Utilizing Adobe and Microsoft Publishing Software

ACKNOWLEDGMENTS

First, I would like to thank God because without Him, His Son Jesus Christ and through the Holy Spirit, I could have never done this. I would like to thank my husband Ronald Ballard Jr. for his love, continual prayers and constant support. My beautiful daughter MoNae L. Lewis who understood most of the time and always told me daily I had the key to her heart.

I want to thank all my family and friends, especially my daddy Cleveland Scott Jr., Carolyn Ballard, Ronald Ballard Sr., Diana Maria Avery-Kerns, my sisters Larenda, Sharnika, and Marquita, my brother Cleveland, Sister in Law Tanya, Anthony Gaddy, Mark Flowers, Derran, Nate, Juanita, Regina, Bob, Tony Crawford, Miguel, Derrick, William, Angela, Nadine, Milton, Jack, Tiffany, Detrick, Dayan, Brandon, Justin, Rocky, Ronesha, Rache', Gwen, Maurice, Warren, Denise (Neicy), Rache', Denia, Tamika, Mark, Jianae, Tymir, Jaden, Kaprice, Robert (RJ), Xavier, all my nieces and nephews.

To my Late Great-Great Grandmother Sarah Glover, The Late Great Grandmother Annie Williams, The Late Great Grandma Jean, The Late Catherine Lewis (Nana), The Late Viola Merriman (Mom Vi), The Late Bernice Wright (Nana), my Great Grandmother Hattie Scott, Grandmothers Ellen Scott (Mother), Claudine Starks. My Grandfathers Eugene Starks, The Late Cleveland Scott Sr., The Late William Glover, The Late Arthur Glover, The Late Charles Wright, The Late Charles Lewis and Sister in Law The Late Miriam Lewis-Valentine and The Late Michael Francis, Dr. Myria Mack-Williams.

To Senior Pastor David Pope and First Lady Terri Pope of New Life International Church, you are a true blessing! I cannot thank you enough for your special encouragement and prayers. You help elevate my poetry and spiritual gifts to the next level and help me give God my very best. You have

ACKNOWLEDGMENTS

been a mentor and a spiritual covering for me and my family for over three years and I ask God to bless you from the depths of my soul. You Pastor Pope took a special interest in my spiritual gifts and helped me develop them and continue to do so. Having me perform with Clifton Davis was an honor, and God Gets the Glory! You and your wife are two beautiful people and I am glad God brought you into our lives! To my second mom, Pastor Ethelynn Taylor, who presented me with a special Bible on March 17, 2001. What I remember most is what she wrote inside: Isaiah 40:8 "The Grass withers and the flowers fade but the Word of our GOD STANDS FOREVER!" This book is also in memory of your son and my friend The Late Harold Taylor "Herbie". I miss you and I will always love you.

DEDICATIONS

I dedicate this book back to God and His Son Jesus Christ, who is my Savior! I also want to thank God for His Holy Spirit and my spiritual gifts! I love You so much!

Also, I dedicate this book to my best friend, my mother Jean A. Scott. Mommy, I thank you from the bottom of my heart. You are my biggest cheerleader; you encouraged me, prayed for me, dried my tears, held me in your arms, and listened to all my poems!

Mom

There are no real words to truly express

My deepest thoughts or feelings,

I have in my heart for you.

Except to say "I Love You" and

I'm thankful to God that

He chose you for my mother and

For that I am very blessed.

There is nothing in this world

That's more precious than you.

You are my mother but more like my sister.

You're my very best friend.

Kitten

Thank you for the support—Daddy (Cleveland Scott Jr.), my husband, Ronald Ballard Jr., and my beautiful daughter MoNae L. Lewis this book is also dedicated to you.

TABLE OF CONTENTS

Introduction..	i
My Prayer..	01
Angels are our Protector..	03
Keep Blessing My Soul with Music........................	05
Count Your Blessings...	07
The Ten Commandments.......................................	08
My Body Was Healed...	10
Hold On!...	12
Daddy...	14
Dad..	15
Mother...	16
I'm Turning to God...	17
Go to God for Protection from Abuse....................	18
Dr. Martin Luther King, Jr.......................................	19
Psalm 116, 1-1-14...	20
Have Faith...	21
Examine Your Heart...	22
The Bible is Your Sword..	24
Grandparents Taking Care of Their Grandchildren.....	26
The Second Time Around......................................	28

TABLE OF CONTENTS

Peace for the World.	29
Sadness of the World.	30
Thanksgiving is the Time of Year.	31
Church is What We Need.	33
Caring for Others.	34
Thank You for Being You.	35
A Childs Birth.	37
Arguments Hurt.	38
My Husband, My Lover, My Friend.	39
Child Abuse (My True Story).	40
A Burden I am Carrying.	41
An Encouraging Word for You.	42
Matthew 6:1-12 (KVJ) How to Pray.	43
Look Out for the Elderly.	46
Mommy and Me.	47
God's Gift, It's A Miracle.	48
Let It Go.	49
Preparing for Baptism.	51
Listen My Friend.	54
Give, Give, Give.	56
Give Your Tithes and Offers with Joy.	57

TABLE OF CONTENTS

Your Soul	58
Generosity	59
Being Single is Not a Curse	60
Depression (An Illness or A Generational Curse?)	62
Holiday Blues	63
A Broken Heart	64
The Lords Prayer, Psalm 23	65
CHRISTMAS	66
Pray for Our Government	68
Suicide is Not the Way Out!	70
Why Do I Celebrate Easter	72
Do You Believe?	73
Where are You Going?	74
Closing Prayer	75

INTRODUCTION

God has blessed my mother and I with the spiritual gift of writing poetry. Through my lifetime, I had experiences like most people where God had to cover me. He was the only one I could depend on to get me through the roughest times of my life. That's when I found poetry. I didn't know my mother was writing poetry also. But one thing is for sure, I felt better every time I wrote my feelings down!

I was lying in the bed and could not move from pain, with tears flowing from my eyes, God told me to pick up a pen and write. And I did what God said, (that is being obedient) and writing one poem led to two and so on. Then I fell asleep, and a vision appeared in my dreams just as clear as if I was watching a television show. I was writing a book. Therefore I jumped up from my sleep and started writing down everything I saw in my dream, so I would not forget anything! Then I prayed! That's how God works! Then two days later I received a telephone call from a special Deacon to check up on me and have prayer. She asked me to document everything in a journal and that was a confirmation of my dreams...Praise God!

When I called my mother the next morning, she was already writing poetry (as I said earlier), and we then started doing God's work!

My only true purpose for writing this book is for healing, and that people learn about God and His Son Jesus Christ who my mother and I love so very much. I also pray that someone, everyone get saved! My mother and I have such an awesome relationship with God and His Son Jesus and we want that for you. We really don't care what your faith is, God loves everyone!

My Prayer

Heavenly Father, I say thank you.

Thank you for this gift of poetry,

To spread some love and to encourage others through ministry.

My prayer is that people's lives will be touched,

And through our poetry it will also heal their hearts.

I thank you God for spiritual gifts,

I thank you most for the gift of poetry because;

Writing my true feelings down saved my life.

Therefore, God you are first on my list.

I thank you for your Son Jesus Christ, my Savior.

I found Him a long time ago.

No words could ever express how much, I love you Both so.

Heavenly Father, I will serve You with my entire heart and

I will praise You until I take my last breath.

You have covered me, no matter what life has dealt,

I am truly blessed.

Once again, I say thank you.

In Jesus' name I pray. Amen.

John 16:23-24

Pray in Jesus' name.

Angels are our Protectors

Daniel 6:22

Angels Protect God's People.

Angels are our Protectors

Angels are a blessing; we all know this is true.

They are here to carry out God's plan,

They will pass judgment on you.

Angels should not be worshiped, but they are Holy;

And we are thankful for them too.

Angels are here to serve God only;

They are also here to give protection to you.

Angels are sent to surround you,

Angels are God's messengers.

Angels are with the Heavenly Father;

And on earth watching over you.

Our Heavenly Father has given all of us a gift;

He assigned each one of us angels, for you and for me.

Daniel 6:22

Angels Protect God's People.

Keep Blessing My Soul with Music
(Music is a Special Gift from God)

The passion I feel when I hear my favorite song, it runs so deep; I Jump so high in church, out of my seat. I no longer feel my legs; thank God I land on my feet!

Exodus 15:1

Music can be used to worship God.

Keep Blessing My Soul with Music

How music makes me feel, no words can express,
How music soothes my soul and brings me happiness.

Music is a special gift from God,
It has been a blessing to my life
Just to hear the choir sing takes away my pain.

I love music; it helps me when I'm going through sadness or stress.
I love to worship God so much through music,
It is very difficult for me to explain it to you.

The passion I feel when I hear my favorite song,
It runs so deep; I Jump so high in church, out of my seat;
I no longer feel my legs; thank God I land on my feet!

Therefore, you awesome gospel singers I want to encourage you,
To keep blessing my soul with music and doing God's work too!

This is dedicated to: Evangelist Serena Ford, Judy Peterson, MAKEDA, Shirley Caesar, Risen, Susan Coe, Cece Winas, Yolanda Adams, Kym Branch, Donnie McClurkin, Fred Hammond, Kirk Franklin, John P. Kee, Set Apart, Terrell Guy, DJ & Lisa, to name a few...Thank you!

Exodus 15:1
Music can be used to worship God.

Colossians 3:16
We should make music for God's glory.

Count Your Blessings

Count Your Blessings, If you have a roof over your head. Someone is also looking to keep warm and a box for their bed.

This could be you!

Always, Count Your Blessings!

**Psalm 5:12
God blesses Righteous People.**

Count Your Blessings

Don't worry about what you don't have today.
Count your blessings for what you do have,
And thank God when you pray.

Also, be thankful that you woke up this morning;
And were able to breathe.
Because someone did not wake up from their sleep.

Count Your Blessings,
If you have food on your table to eat.
Because someone out there is looking for food on the street.

Count Your Blessings,
If you have a roof over your head.
Someone is also looking to keep warm and for a box for their bed.

Count your blessings, because this could be you!
So NEVER take life's blessings for granted,
When God has been good to you!

Remember to remain faithful and obey His Commandments.
God and His Holy Angels will continue to cover and protect you!
Always, Count Your Blessings!

Psalm 5:12
God blesses Righteous People.

The Ten Commandments

And God spoke all these words, saying: 'I am the LORD your God...

ONE: 'You shall have no other gods before Me.'

TWO: 'You shall not make for yourself a carved image--any likeness of anything that is in heaven above, or that is in the earth beneath, or that is in the water under the earth.'

THREE: 'You shall not take the name of the LORD your God in vain.'

FOUR: 'Remember the Sabbath day, to keep it Holy.'

FIVE: 'Honor your father and your mother.'

SIX: 'You shall not murder.'

SEVEN: 'You shall not commit adultery.'

EIGHT: 'You shall not steal.'

NINE: 'You shall not bear false witness against your neighbor.'

TEN: 'You shall not covet your neighbor's house; you shall not covet your neighbor's wife, or his male servant, or his female servant, or his ox, or his donkey, or anything that is your neighbor's.

My Body Was Healed

I suffered enough for everyone.

My body was healed, THANK GOD!

Matthew 4:23-25

Don't let Stress cause you to worry.

Jesus can heal sickness.

My Body Was Healed

You can manage stress, instead of it managing you.

I know it's not always easy, but if you don't stress can;

And will hurt you!

Stress equals Worry

Worry equals Pain

Stress can equal the Shingles

The Shingles can equal Death

That's where my story begins

Stress can bring on headaches, stomach pain,

And heart attacks to name a few…

Stress is a serious issue that takes time to learn what to do,

Because I suffered enough for everyone.

Therefore, I was hoping to help people see;

That stress can be defeated through, My Testimony!

I pray every time I have a problem,

I take it straight to God and leave my problem there!

Lately, I show no emotion…I act like I don't even care.

I do my very best to fix what I can, the rest I put in God's hands.

Next, I make sure I exercise, because this is wise.

I eat right, take vitamins, and get plenty of rest,

And cut any negativity out of my life!

Make sure you love God and have plenty of faith.

(Continued)

My Body Was Healed

Then when you feel stress,

Put on your favorite gospel CD; watch your favorite show on TV,

Call a positive friend, go to worship, read the Word or

Just simply fall on your face, after all it's that mean Old Devil (Satan)

We are trying to chase.

Remember, some stressful things are suppose to happen to you.

So you must hold on and don't let life make you Ill.

I'm telling you this for a reason,

Because all things happen to us just for a season.

Stress almost was the death of me.

The doctors say...I am a miracle!

Therefore, I had to let the world know.

Although stress could have killed me,

My God said NO!

I have a purpose for you daughter,

It is NOT your time to go!

Now, can't you see why I won't do anything less?

But, serve God only and refuse to serve stress!

My body was healed, THANK GOD!

Psalm 69:1-36
Pray to God in times of stress.

Hold On!

Hold On!

Especially when it hurts.

Hold On!

Even if you have to cry.

Hold On!

Especially when days seem dark.

Hold On!

When you're all alone.

Hold On!

When all the bills are due.

Hold On!

When there's nothing else you can do.

Just Hold On!!!

Our Father in Heaven will see you through!

I Thessalonians 4:18
We should encourage each other.

Genesis 15:6
Believing God takes faith.

The Late-Arthur Glover

The Late-Arthur Glover and Claudine Starks

In loving memory of my father

Love, Jean A. Glover-Scott

1 Thessalonians 4:13-14

Death is not the end of a person.

Daddy

I thank God for you staying by my side,
And helping me through my daily pain of losing you.

Thank you daddy for keeping us together.
Back in the day, in hard times;
Keeping five children together was not easy to do.

Thank you for the love and care,
Thank you daddy for being there!

I know you're not here today,
But in my heart your love,
And memories will always stay!

I was blessed to have precious time,
To spend with you although you were Ill.
Time that I will never forget.

And as long as I have breath...I will love you.
You have a piece of my heart today and you always will!

In loving memory of my father, the Late-Arthur Glover
Your daughter, Jean A. Glover-Scott

1 Thessalonians 4:13-14
Death is not the end of a person.

Dad

My heart still hurts when I think of you.
You are loved and I truly miss you.
Some days the tears fill my eyes,
And I just break down and cry.

Then I think of the all the memories,
And the times I shared with you.
That brings a smile to my face because…
Dad I'm so glad God picked you for me,
And for our beautiful loving family.

You are so special to me dad.
I'll always keep you deep within my heart.
Therefore, each day I can take you with me.
So, Dad we will never be apart.

In loving memory of my dad, Cleveland Scott, Sr.
Your loving daughter, Linda Scott Roberts
Dedicated Christmas 2004 by: Kitten and Jean

"Happy Fathers Day"

Dads you are loved and we are very proud of your commitment to your family! Remember you are the head of the household and you must always set an example and be a leader! Also, don't leave prayer out! Single fathers, keep up the good work, God has your back! We love you!

I Thessalonians 4:13-18

We sorrow over believers, who die, but one day we will meet again.

Mother

I thank you and I want you to know, how much I love you so.

You have been there for me through the storms and the rain,

Also through good times and the pain.

The beautiful memories, all the caring, sharing;

You're always giving, that still remains.

Even when I lost my way, you still loved me the same.

That's why I have a special place in my heart for you.

I have a need everyday to call and say,

I love you Mother and may God build a fence around you each day

You fed me when I was hungry;

You gave me a place to lay my head

Thank you again for everything you did!

God sent me an angel and the angel was you.

Now, the most important thing to me is;

Keeping God first in my life and my family!

Dedicated to Ellen Scott "Mother" and my mother Claudine

Love, Jean

"Happy Mother's Day"

Mothers you are so special to us and to God!

I Timothy 5:3-5

Families should take care of each other.

I'm Turning to God

I'm turning to God because you hurt me so bad.

I don't know if I will survive this pain.
Nevertheless,
Time has shown me, you are not the man I married.

It seems when things don't go your way,
You take it out on me.
I am going to have to get away,
This situation it's getting worse each day.

I'm turning to God, now.
This is the only thing left, I know now to do!

If I keep going down this road,
My family will be burying ME!

Ephesians 5: 21-6:4
Abuse has no place in family relationships.

Go to God for Protection from Abuse

Father in Heaven,
I need prayer today.

My husband beats me constantly,
He stays out nights and sometimes days.

I am suffering and I don't know what to do?
I have children by this man…I am afraid if I leave him,
He will find me and beat me AGAIN!

Father,

Help me please!
I want to be free of him and all of these bad memories.
I am asking Heavenly Father, have mercy on me.

Find me a way OUT!
From this man who abuses me!

In Jesus' name, I pray Amen

Psalm 12:5
God protects those who are helpless.

Dr. Martin Luther King, Jr.

"I have a dream," said Dr. Martin Luther King, Jr.

These words are embedded in our hearts and soul,

Because we understood his goal.

A goal for peace, love, unity and non-violence for all.

God gave this man a beautiful ministry,

Also a unique and courageous call.

His life's journey will always be remembered.

We were honored to have him,

As a Civil Rights Leader, Preacher and Teacher.

We salute The Late Dr. Martin Luther King, Jr.,

His wife Coretta Scott-King and his family

Congratulations Dr. King on the progress and your life's journey.

I am delighted as we celebrate your memory and as a tribute with a holiday!

Most importantly, it's the history that I'm most proud of,

I am just so grateful that I have the opportunities I have today!

Matthew 5:9

Blessed are the peacemakers, for they shall be called sons of God.

Psalm 116, 1-14

1 I love the LORD, for he heard my voice; he heard my cry for mercy.

2 Because he turned his ear to me, I will call on him as long as I live.

3 The cords of death entangles me, the anguish of the grave came upon me; I was overcome by trouble and sorrow.

4 Then I called on the name of the Lord: "O LORD, SAVE ME!"

5 The LORD is gracious and righteous; our God is full of compassion.

6 The LORD protects the simple hearted; when I was in great need, he saved me.

7 Be at rest once more, O my soul, for the LORD has been good to YOU.

8 For you, O LORD, have delivered my soul from death, my eyes from tears, my feet from stumbling,

9 that I may walk before the LORD in the land of the living.

10 I believed; therefore I said, I am greatly afflicted."

11 And in my dismay I said, "All men are liars."

12 How can I repay the LORD for all his goodness to me?

13 I will lift up the cup of salvation and call on the name of the LORD.

14 I will fulfill my vows to the LORD in the presence of all his people.

Praise the LORD!

Have Faith

To have faith, you must have trust in God.

When you don't have faith, everyone knows it;

And that's a fact, you cannot hide.

You walk around scared, upset, crying, praying,

Trying to figure things out saying, "I don't know what to do?"

The entire time God had it all worked out for you.

See that's how faith works!

God puts you through a test, to see what you are going to do.

In fact, He already knows what is best for you.

Child of God, all of us will be tested in life, for this will make us grow.

Now that you have the secret, you must tell everyone that you know!

So remember, to have "Faith"

No matter what you're going through.

Because the God you serve,

HE would NEVER abandon you!

Matthew 17:20

Keep your faith, as small as a mustard seed.

Hebrews 11:6

And without faith it is impossible to please God, because anyone who comes to him must believe that he exists and that he rewards those who earnestly seek him.

Examine Your Heart

The heart is an organ, yes this is true.
It's also the organ, that shows the real you.
The heart tells the true picture; if you are real or fake.
It helps with discernment on the friends and decisions you should make.

If you are not careful, sometimes the heart plays tricks on you.
You get deceived and get a heartbreak or two.
Nevertheless, if your heart is real, then God will know this for a fact.
Just keep repenting for your sins and Our Father in Heaven has your back!

Then when this life is over and it is all said and done,
If your name is written in the Book of Life.
You, my dear, will forever live with God and His Son.
Most importantly, the victory will have been won!

Always examine your heart daily.
Be kind, show love, and respect to others and accept Jesus Christ,
Before it's too late!

Your goal in life is to accept Jesus as your Savior to be with Him;
And His Father when He returns, and to enter Heaven's gates!

1 Samuel 16:7

But the Lord said to Samuel, "Do not look at his appearance or his physical stature, because I have refused him. For the Lord does not see as man sees; for man looks at the outward appearance, but the Lord looks at the heart."

The Bible is Your Sword

Just take the Bible with you, it's your protection and sword,

This is not coming from me, Thus Sayeth the Lord!

2 Timothy 3:16-17

All scripture is **God-breathed** and is useful for teaching, rebuking, correcting and training in righteousness, so that the man of God may be thoroughly equipped for every good work.

The Bible is Your Sword

I read my Bible everyday because I learn something new.
It's wonderful to read what God has to say.
The Bible is our tool on earth to teach us;
God's Law, His Commandments, how to pray, about His prophets;
And especially about His Son.

If you are reading my poetry book, God bless you!
And thank you, but if you don't have a Holy Bible;
Please, my dear, go and buy one!

The Bible is the most important book that you could ever have.
It also builds your personal relationship with God and Jesus Christ His Son.
The Bible gives you knowledge and power,
To face life's storms that comes your way.
Reading the Bible makes you feel good inside,
Especially when you learn a scripture that makes your day.

Finally, take your Bible with you.
That's why it's good to have at least two.
Take it to church, to the supermarket, the movies, everywhere you go.
You never know when you are going to need it.
Need it for yourself or someone else to share God's Word,
For the Bible is your sword!

God and Jesus is a Spirit.
They are in your heart but the Bible is with you physically.
(I think you get the picture I am trying to get you to see)

(Continued)

The Bible is Your Sword!

You can see it, feel it, and open it to your favorite part.
Just use it to minister to someone's soul,
To encourage them or just read it in your spare time.

Just take the Bible with you,
It's your protection and sword,
This is not coming from me, Thus Sayeth the Lord!

2 Timothy 3:16-17
All scripture is God-breathed and is useful for teaching, rebuking, correcting and training in righteousness, so that the man of God may be thoroughly equipped for every good work.

(And so can you)

This is dedicated:
To my Bishop S. Todd Townsend who taught me to
Always carry my sword. (The Holy Bible)

There are many versions other than the original King James. I found for myself The New King James, NIV (New International Version) and the New Living Translation Holy Bible are easier to read and understand, also please encourage your children to read their Bibles also.

Remember they follow by example. God Bless You!

Grandparents Taking Care of Their Grandchildren

Grandparents who are raising their grandchildren,
My heart goes out to you because I know this is not an easy thing to do.

You are one of God's angels, taking care of these children.
Whose little eyes at night look up to you or they may need to be held,
Helped with homework, just loved,
You know what God placed you here to do.
There are so many of you out there. I know this to be true.

I am sending this encouragement,
When times get difficult, just keep holding on.
These children are so blessed to have you in their lives.

You are now mommy or daddy, and these children need you.
We are Thankful for your love, patience and willingness to step in.
For I know these children are grateful, because you put a smile on their face.
Also, you are someone they can depend on in their life;
And you grandparents cannot be replaced; my prayers go out to you.

And I have nothing but admiration, my hat goes off to you!
God knows and sees what you're doing for the grandchildren.
Teach them the Word, and let them know that both God,
And Jesus love them too then you truly will be rewarded in heaven,
When you do God's will, He has a place In His Kingdom especially for you!

Hebrews 13:16

But do not forget to do good and to share, for with such sacrifices God is well pleased.

The Second Time Around

Mr. and Mrs. Ronald Ballard Jr.
Married on October 10, 1999

This man will be a blessing and he will be a Man of God.

He will be your greatest friend, fulfilling your every need.

Ephesians 5:25
Husbands love your wives just as Christ also loved the church and gave Himself for her.

Proverbs 18:22
He who finds a wife finds a good thing and obtains favor from the Lord.

Second Time Around

When your first love hurt you, you may cry, day and night.
The hurt is so unbearable, you feel as if you want to give up and die.

Then someone comes in your life and shows you how to love again,
With tenderness and kindness, that is usually how it starts.
Trust me, you will know, listen to your heart.

As time passes, God will reveal the truth, if this is the man for you;
Your broken heart, He will heal.

This man will be a blessing and he will be a Man of God.
He will be your greatest friend, fulfilling your every need.

Doing everything he can, to show you how to love again.
You must be patient, for God can only bless you with this gift.
You can be happy and truly in love.

The Second Time Around

Ephesians 5:25
Husbands, love your wives just as Christ also loved the church and gave Himself for her.

Proverbs 18:22
He who finds a wife finds a good thing and obtains favor from the Lord.

Peace for the World

Pray for love, pray for peace,
Pray for the men and women fighting overseas.
Pray for their mothers, fathers, and loved ones who are missing them.

Hoping that this war will be over soon,
So they can come home to their families.
Who are waiting desperately to see them again.

Pray for the men and women, who have lost their lives;
My heart goes out to their families.
No one knows what the family is going through.
Let's just pray, we need to give them a thought everyday.

To the men and women who have paid the price,
Of losing their lives for our FREEDOM, may you Rest in Peace.

We pray that this War will be over soon someday.
Until then, let's continue to pray for them and for peace daily.
Just Pray!

Isaiah 53:5

But He was wounded for our transgressions, He was bruised for our iniquities; the chastisement for our peace was upon Him, and by His stripes we are healed.

Sadness of the World

Pray, for the sadness of the world Innocent children are dying, having their lives taken away from them, Pray for the families whose hearts are in so much pain today. Pray because we are on the outside looking in, for we do not know of the families' true suffering, so just pray.

People are losing their lives, all over the world. Even on the streets here in our cities and in many countries. The sadness of the world, the pain is unreal my heart is overwhelmed with the sorrows and the sadness of the world. There is so much going on that I get so filled up at times, just thinking about this. Let's all pray for peace everyday Also, let's have a special prayer for the men and women in blue fighting in the city streets for our protection daily. The firemen or anyone in harms way the fighting and the lost lives in Africa and The lost lives in the Tsunami, Hurricane Katrina, our men and women in the war overseas and the fighting In the whole country or on our streets daily.

Please, Pray for Peace!

Isaiah 26:3

He will keep you in perfect peace whose mind is steadfast on him.

Thanksgiving is the Time of Year

To give thanks to God for the family that we hold dear,
Thanksgiving is the time that we laugh and show love.
That is why we are thankful for this time to be together,
It is a blessing from above.

It's also a blessing to a have our health and strength,
It's also great to watch TV, have company
Or talk to each other at great length.

Do not forget the food, it's the bomb!
We thank the Lord for Thanksgiving,
Because we the Scott's, the Ballard's and the Lewis Family,
Have a good time!

(Miss you already, Nana, Thanksgiving dinner will never be the same but your memory will live forever, therefore you and Pop Pop will be there in spirit)

Psalm 100:4
Enter into His gates with Thanksgiving, And into His courts with praise. Be Thankful to Him, and bless His name.

Praise the Lord!

Psalm 150:6

Let everything that has breath praise the Lord

Praise the Lord!

Church is What We Need

For us, Church is what we need to be able to praise His name,
And thank the Lord in His house one more time.

We do not know the day, time, or hour;
That we will be saying goodbye.
Therefore, it's a privilege to go church;
That's how my mom and I feel inside.
We are fighting to sit by Jesus' side.

Today, all we want to do is put God first in our lives and live right,
Also be the person God wants us to be on the inside.
And blessed if our light shines on the outside.

Going to church on Sunday or any day;
Touches our soul, our mind, our body and our heart!

We will be going to church until God calls both of us Home.
It is what we desire to do.
We will be praying for the same for the world;
And our loved ones, too!

Psalm 150:6
Let everything that has breath praise the Lord.

Praise the Lord!

Caring for Others

Try each day as much as you can,

To say a kind word or help an elderly person.

Even your family members or friends.

Jesus loves a humble heart,

To give care to others that may not be doing as well as you.

Care for the sick,

Care for some one who's hurting too.

In this lifetime, if you can take time;

Try to do the little things for someone in need.

To give care to anyone, for this God will bless you.

1 Thessalonians 2:7

As apostles of Christ we could have been a burden to you, but we were gentle among you, like a mother caring for her little children.

Thank You for Being You

I know it's been some time since you heard from me;
Honestly, it's been to long and yes, I'm still your best friend.

Friendship is everlasting, no matter how much time has passed.
God brought you in my life to stand the test of time,
The bond we share will last.

Looking back on the memories…WOW, we had a blast!
Some things make me chuckle and some make me laugh.

If I lost you completely, I don't know what I would do,
But, one thing is for sure…
They broke the mold, when they made you!

I will never again take you for granted.
I've learned to have you as a friend,
Is worth more to me than silver or gold.

To have you as a part of my life is a gift from God from above,
For which I am truly blessed.
To sum it all up in just ONE word your friendship is…

Priceless!

Thank you for being you!

Proverbs 18:24
Faithful friends are not common.

A Childs Birth

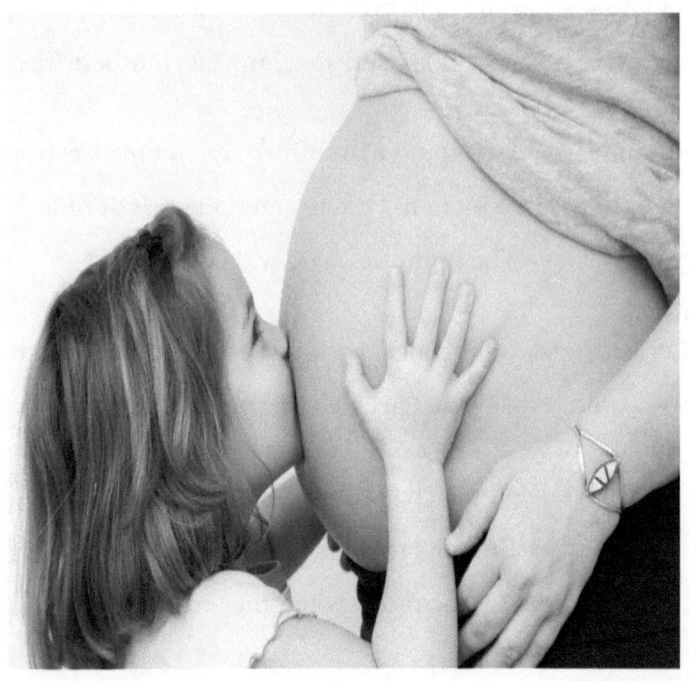

It's A Miracle

**Psalm 127:3-5
Children are a blessing from God.**

A Childs Birth

A child's birth is one of the most beautiful things in the world,
That two people can share.
Hearing those words, "You have a healthy boy or girl."
Brings most mothers' and fathers' eyes to tears!

Holding that little life that you made in your arms
Or passing the blessing to your husband's hands,
Brings a smile to your heart and your face.
The love you feel at that moment,
That special love cannot and will never be replaced.

Again, holding that little beautiful child, or maybe two?
It doesn't matter how many,
A child's birth is a gift from God
And the Angels are smiling down on you.

It's a miracle
Nine months, carrying a life and it is living inside of you.
It's just a miracle to me.

Anyone who has suffered the loss of a child through a miscarriage, stillborn, or a loss of their child shortly after birth due to a medical condition, or whatever the cause: The birth of your child was also a blessing and the memory will live on forever. We are sorry for your loss. Anelda and Jean

Psalm 127:3-5
Children are a blessing from God.

Arguments Hurt

You can't live your life holding on to anger, when arguments hurt.
I know sometimes, when you think people are your true friends,
And then, they end up hurting you.

You must let them go and pray for forgiveness for you don't know,
How much stress, this situation has brought to you;
And the person involved in the argument too.

Arguments hurt but again you must forgive and pray to God;
And through His grace and mercy, He will heal you.

If your name is not written in the Book of Life,
You cannot enter into the Heavenly Gates.

This is ONE argument with God you will lose;
AND YOU CANNOT ESCAPE!

Sorry!

Philippians 2:14
We should avoid arguments.

Proverbs 15:1
Arguments can be avoided by using gentle words.

My Husband, My Lover, My Friend

We've been through storms in this life,
Good times and some bad.

Over the years, our love still remains the same;
It's even gotten better, hotter than any fire or flames.

God has also blessed us with five beautiful kids,
And I am blessed to have you in my life.
A good husband, also father you have been;
Most importantly, a treasured friend.

If I must grade you honey,
You would surely get an A + from me.
As a bonus, you are on the top of my list;
You will always be a special gift.

The way you have always been but, most importantly;
You will be my husband, my lover, and my friend.

Especially written for my husband, Cleveland Scott Jr.

Your loving wife, Jean

Mark 10:2-12

Two people become one through marriage.

Child Abuse
(My True Story)

I need to tell my story,

Hoping that it will help someone heal.

I was abused as a young kid,

I was only four or five years old.

One of my family members took advantage of me;

He came in my room and put his body on top of mine.

I have blocked the memory out, because he did it many times.

Now, I am grown and I ask God for forgiveness of him.

Because, I know now he was sick in his mind;

I also know it is no fault of mine!

If what happened to me, ever happened to you;

Remember, please remember, it is not your fault!

Talk to someone about it, so you can heal.

No matter what they have done,

They had a very sick mind and were totally wrong!

Exodus 22:21

God cares about minorities.

Matthew 6:14-15

We must forgive others.

A Burden I Am Carrying

I have been resting with this burden, for a long time.
One of my children is not my husband's kid.

I have kept this secret tormenting my memory, deep inside of me.
The father of my child has a wife and a family.

I should had never had this affair.
I don't know how to tell my husband,
We have been together for so many years.

I am praying and asking for forgiveness.
Lord, this is the only thing I know how to do.
So now, I am taking this burden from me and giving it to you.

To leave it there!

1 John 1:8-9
God will forgive our sins if we confess them.

An Encouraging Word for You

I want to send an encouraging word your way.

I know that you are hurting and your spirit may be very low today.

Open your heart,

Open your Bible to God's Word,

He will help you find your way.

I know sometimes you think,

You cannot even make it through the day;

And your nights seem so long.

Just remember,

That the Lord can help you and He will.

When you, my dear, open your heart and pray.

When you trust Him and let Him take care of you.

TOMORROW will be better day!

Isaiah 40:31

God encourages us.

Roman 15:4

The bible encourages us.

Matthew 6:1-12 (KJV) How to Pray

¹Take heed that ye do not your alms before men, to be seen of them: otherwise ye have no reward of your Father which is in heaven.

²Therefore when thou doest thine alms, do not sound a trumpet before thee, as the hypocrites do in the synagogues and in the streets, that they may have glory of men. Verily I say unto you, They have their reward.

³But when thou doest alms, let not thy left hand know what thy right hand doeth:

⁴That thine alms may be in secret: and thy Father which seeth in secret himself shall reward thee openly.

⁵And when thou prayest, thou shalt not be as the hypocrites are: for they love to pray standing in the synagogues and in the corners of the streets, that they may be seen of men. Verily I say unto you, They have their reward.

⁶But thou, when thou prayest, enter into thy closet, and when thou hast shut thy door, pray to thy Father which is in secret; and thy Father which seeth in secret shall reward thee openly.

Matthew 6:1-12 (KJV) How to Pray

⁷But when ye pray, use not vain repetitions, as the heathen do: for they think that they shall be heard for their much speaking.

⁸Be not ye therefore like unto them: for your Father knoweth what things ye have need of, before ye ask him.

⁹After this manner therefore pray ye: Our Father which art in heaven, Hallowed be thy name.

¹⁰Thy kingdom come, Thy will be done in earth, as it is in heaven.

¹¹Give us this day our daily bread.

¹²And forgive us our debts, as we forgive our debtors.

¹³And lead us not into temptation, but deliver us from evil: For thine is the kingdom, and the power, and the glory, for ever. Amen.

Alms--money, food, or other donations given to the poor or needy; anything given as charity: *The hands of the beggars were outstretched for alms.*

Look Out for the Elderly

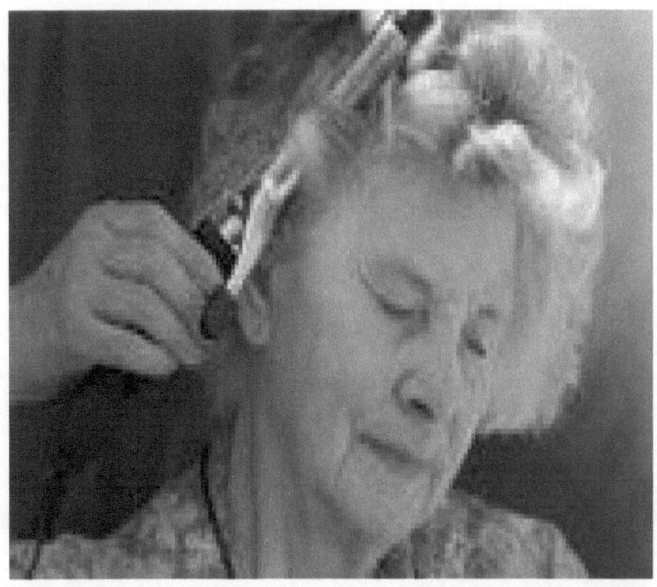

Bless the elderly, some may need a friend. Sometimes they just need a kind word, or someone to talk to them.

Psalm 68:6

God takes care of lonely people.

Look Out for the Elderly

Please whatever you do, look out for the elderly.
One day you may be blessed to be one.
God bless the elderly, for some are lonely.
The elderly may need someone to look after them.

Some are ill and some need people to service them.
Bless the elderly, some may need a friend.
Sometimes they just need a kind word,
Or someone to talk to them.

If you know of an elderly person living all alone,
Open your heart to them and call them on the phone.
You will be surprised of the blessing that will come to you.

God Bless the Elderly

You might be surprised of the wisdom they can give to you.

God Bless the Elderly

I found out that some people have been hurting the elderly,
I am ashamed of you, please stop and give them respect.
Do what Jesus would do!
Whoever you are, may God have mercy on you.

Genesis 2:18
God is concerned about our loneliness.

Mommy and Me

Thank you for everything you do for me.
Taking care of me and teaching me to be the best I can be.

There's not a day that goes by that I don't think of you,
You give me your all in everything you do.

Mommy, I love you.
Mommy, from the depths of my heart,
May God bless you.

Daddy is not here in our life, I wish he could be.
Now I pray, that God takes care of you;
Because now, it's just Mommy and Me.

Exodus 20:12
God tells children to honor their parents.

God's Gift, It's A Miracle

Mommy, It's Me
I started as just a little seed,
In the womb growing day by day.

Mommy,
Tell daddy and the family that in a few months
They will see me; soon I'll be on my way.

I'm God's gift; I'm your miracle that God is going to give to you.
Mommy, lean not your own understanding;
Just trust God because my life and your life are in His hands.

I ask Jesus during my birth,
Please, take care of my mommy and me

Mommy, Jesus is still showing the world,
That He is alive and well.
Jesus is still performing miracles.

I'm a miracle mommy, a blessing from above,
God's gift mommy, the blessings is ME "LOVE"

Job 5:9
He does great things too marvelous to understand. He performs countless miracles.

LET IT GO

If it's hurting you, Let It Go!

Don't let the past consume you,

Because, memories will haunt you and drive you crazy.

So, if it is hurting you, Let It Go!

Trust me when I tell you,

I know this is difficult but you have NO other choice,

But, to live and to Let It Go!

Remember, if you are a Child of God;

Then forgiveness should be enough!

Just pray for them and concentrate on yourself.

Read Isaiah 26:3

He will keep you in perfect peace

Whose mind is steadfast on Him.

Our God gives us Scripture to help you in life with problems,

And help you solve them.

Also, to be closer to you than a mother, father or a very best friend.

As this poem comes to an end,

There is one thing you must know!

Give everything, every hurt, and every care to the Lord,

Because He hears and He cares, then leave it there,

And…Let it Go!

"Take Me to the Water to be Baptized"

"Take Me to the Water to be Baptized." We all know that favorite hymn. Baptism is one of the most beautiful ceremonies I have ever seen. *Congratulations to Joseph Ashe on making the decision to get baptized and MoNae (my daughter) she got baptized on March 2, 2005,*

Mark 1:9
Jesus was baptized

Preparing for Baptism

"Take Me to the Water to be Baptized."
We all know that favorite hymn.
Baptism is one of the most beautiful ceremonies I have ever seen.
I love to help the candidates prepare for baptism.

A lot of people are afraid of being baptized or
Think it is just a ceremony, so it's not necessary.

Well, If Jesus thought it was necessary,
Then you must re-think your decision and get baptized!

Baptism means throwing away the old person and becoming a new person spiritually. You have accepted Jesus as your Savior and you are doing this in public for your family, friends, and whoever comes to see. You are just going to try to live the best Christian life you can, be Christ like, but do not think just because you got baptized the old you won't creep up!

That's why we work on it daily. It is a lifetime commitment.
MoNae (my daughter) got baptized on March 2, 2005,
I love you and mommy is proud of you.

The Baptismal Ceremony is this Simple:

(I am sure every church or ceremony is different)

(Continued)

Preparing for Baptism

1. You are prayed for and asked some questions about your Savior JESUS CHRIST.

2. You get dressed in all white, including underclothes, T-shirts, a bathing cap (for women and little girls to protect their hair), and baptismal gowns.

3. You are escorted to the Sanctuary to line up, while beautiful music is playing.

4. You are escorted to the Baptismal Pool.

5. In the Baptismal Pool, there are normally two people. (One Pastor and one Deacon for Assistance) Remember I am sure every church or ceremony is different.

6. You are helped into the Baptismal Pool by another escort (Deacon).

7. Once inside the Baptismal Pool, the Pastor or the assistant (Deacon) will tell you to hold your breath (you may also want to hold your nose), while placing his hand on your back for support and possibly the back of your head. The assisting Deacon will also be holding you with his hands for firm support. **(You are about to be baptized—relax you are God's child)**

8. You will hear the Preacher/Pastor say, "I baptize you in the name of the Father, the Son and the Holy Spirit."

(Continued)

Preparing for Baptism (Part 3)

9. Then they both will put you under the water quickly, about a second or two.

10. You will hear applause because we are proud of you.

11. Next, you are handed a towel and will be escorted out of the Baptismal Pool by an escort (Deacon).
Note: You may feel cold from the water, don't let that alarm you.

12. Now, you are BAPTIZED!

CONGRATULATIONS PRAISE THE LORD!

You are immediately received by a Deacon to change back into your dry clothes, and then you return to the rest of the
Baptismal Ceremony!

It is normally good to get baptized when you understand it and
When you want to **(or feel the Holy Spirit telling you to).**
Never be forced to get baptized. Ask Questions! It is best to get baptized before the age thirteen. Thirteen is the age when sins count on you, but you can do it at any age, just don't be afraid.

This is dedicated to my daughter MoNae Lewis
Congratulations on your baptism on March 02, 2005I Love You!

Matthew 3:11
Baptism signifies repentance.

Listen My Friend

If you want to succeed this is what I want to say…

You must put God first,

Read God's Word, and always pray morning, noon and night.

Be good to all people; treat your parents, guardians, and elders right.

Make sure you accept the Lord as your Savior,

And let The Holy Spirit guide your steps.

Get your education,

Now, you are on the right track!

There is one (1) more thing that most people do not have a clue about,

Unfortunately, It may be hurting you.

It is really easy as 1, 2, 3

Just hit the remote control or push a button

And Turn off the TV!

Joshua 1:7-8 (Whole Chapter)

Be strong and very courageous. Be careful to obey all the law my servant Moses gave you; do not turn from it to the right or to the left, that you may be successful wherever you go. 8. Do not let this Book of the Law depart from your mouth; meditate on it day and night, so that you may be careful to do everything written in it. Then you will be prosperous and successful.

Give, Give, Give

Give, Give, Give

A smile, a hug, or a compliment;
Because it may make someone's day.

1 John 3:17
Giving reflects God's love.

Give, Give, Give

A smile, a hug, or a compliment;
Because it may make someone's day.

Give, Give, Give

After all God gave His Son, so we can live.

Give, Give, Give

It warms your heart and it feels you with gladness.

Give, Give, Give

That is what the world needs.
When you give a smile or hug, it does not cost a thing!
It's always better to give than receive.

Give, Give, Give

1 John 3:17
Giving reflects God's love.

Give Your Tithes and Offering with Joy

Give your tithes and offering with and joy,
You will be blessed, this I guarantee.

Do not give your tithes and offering with malice;
In your heart, for this is not the way to give.
Give back to the Lord and He will return double to you.
Hold on to faith and watch the miracle;
While your sky turns from gray to blue.

Only 10% of your earnings,
God asks that you to return to Him.
This is not much, you must agree,

Be obedient to God's Word
Please remember, that you reap what you sow,
When you sow your seed, your faith and your ministry does GROW!

Ask me, I know, I have a personal testimony
God is faithful when we are faithful

Malachi 3:10

Bring all the tithes into the storehouse so there will be enough food in my temple. "If you do," says the LORD Almighty, "I will open the windows of heaven for you. I will pour out a blessing so great you won't have enough room to take in! Try it! Let me prove it to you!"

Your Soul

People cannot destroy your soul,

Once you have accepted Christ as your Lord and Savior;

Which is worth more than silver or gold.

It is no value to gain the world but lose your soul.

Jesus Christ will be your protection of your heart, mind, and soul.

This message is clear for the rich, poor, young and old.

So whatever you do, this much is true…

When God calls your name,

There is nothing material you can take with you.

So please, accept Jesus Christ as your personal Savior,

This will make you have Eternal Life.

Again,

I guarantee Jesus Christ will protect your heart, mind and soul.

Mark 8:34-38

It is of no value to gain the world but lose your soul.

GENEROSITY

Whoever takes up the burden of his neighbor,
And minister's to those in need;
I want to thank you for your generosity, love and kindness;
You have lightened their burdens and pleased God by doing a good deed.

You gave them hope and hope is the belief that joy will come again.
You became more than a neighbor, you became a friend.

A true friend has a generous heart,
And a generous heart, gives whatever they have freely;
With no strings attached.

Not necessarily money or anything of value,
But words of encouragement, sympathy, love, wisdom and or understanding.
Also, expecting nothing in return; expecting nothing back.

The generous prosper and are satisfied.
Giving is generous and is one secret of being happy,
Whether you give something large or small.
If you give, you will receive…
This is a message from God to you all.

Luke 6:38

Give and it will be given to you: good measure, pressed down, shaken together, and running over will be put into you bosom. For with the same measure that you use, it will be measured back to you."

Being Single is Not a Curse

Being single is not a curse; it's a call from God to do His work.
I know there are days when you pray for a spouse,
But, God knows what is best,
For only He knows the true plan for your life.

There is a message, which is clear.
If you are not living right because being single is hard,
And fighting your flesh is a fight…

Singles, God made sex for marriage, just ask me how I know;
Most importantly, it's for your protection also.
So, wait for marriage.

Ask the women, who got their hearts broken,
Because they didn't marry their first.
Or, the women who got AIDS from their lover,
And infected their unborn sons or the women who got Chlamydia,
And it turned to PID.
Let's stop beating around the bush, just ask me!
Also, I was not single, so there is still risk with unprotected sex.
Unfortunately!

Matthew 19:12
Some people remain single to work for God's Kingdom.

Proverbs 5:15-21
Sex is God's gift to married people.

Depression (An Illness or a Generational Curse?)

Then get on your knees and pray, take the depression to God

I command that depression to leave!

Revelation 21:4

God will wipe away depression.

Depression (An Illness or A Generational Curse?)

Depression…Is it a mental illness or a generational curse?
This question many people ask, but can't always agree upon.
But depression does exist and it is serious too.

This subject is dear to my heart;
Therefore, I want to talk about it so it may help you.

Depression is a subject most people like to keep a secret,
Until is much too late.

Most people are embarrassed, especially if they are saved.
They feel this way, while some just cry and others just pray.
Depression is not an emotion that we should ignore or put aside.

My friend, if you ever have thoughts of hurting yourself by taking pills,
Or other ways of committing suicide, this is one emotion,
You should not hide!
Please call for help, call 911

Then get on your knees and pray, take that depression to God.
For He already knows and is on your side
Trust in Him when you feel down and low,
On your knees is sometimes the only place you can go.
Remember if you believe, you will receive!
I command that depression to leave!

Revelation 21:4
God will wipe away depression.

Holiday Blues

If holidays make you sad,
If that is how you feel?
Then this is dedicated to you.

I know you think that no one understands,
Why you should not be feeling down or feeling blue.

You may have cried all night long,
Or turned down an invitation or two.
If everyone really searched their heart,
Once in your life this just may have been you.

I just want you to know,
No matter what your holiday is missing:
Loss of a love one, no money, no job, or you didn't get a special treat.
You are still blessed when you woke up this morning or had food;
And had a warm place to sleep.

Sometimes our memories will just have to do.
So on the next holiday if you are sad,
Or having difficulty making it through,
You pray for me and I'll pray for you.

2 Corinthians 1:5-11
God comforts those who are hurting.

A Broken Heart

How can you evangelize to someone who has A Broken Heart?
How can you convenience them that Jesus Christ is the Answer,
When their life has been torn apart?

How do you tell someone that the sun will shine again?
When all they see is hopelessness as soon as night turns dark?

How do you start to mend A Broken Heart?
Go to your Heavenly Father in Prayer that is where you start!

Life gets hard sometimes and gets you down,
Nevertheless, God can turn any situation around,
But, It may take time to Heal, in God's time it Will

You must believe in order to receive,
God's blessings and love that is sent from Above

You are A Child of God, therefore your Heart is in His Care and
It will be mended, when you give Him the PAIN and leave it there!

How you mend A Broken Heart?
Is not simple or easy,
I understand because I have been there!

That is how I know that God and His Son Jesus Christ is the only ONE'S
That TRULY CARES!

Psalm 34:18

God heals those with broken hearts.

The Lords Prayer

Psalm 23 (New King James Version)

A Psalm of David.

1 The LORD *is* my shepherd;

I shall not want.

2 He makes me to lie down in green pastures;

He leads me beside the still waters.

3 He restores my soul;

He leads me in the paths of righteousness

For His name's sake.

4 Yea, though I walk through the valley of the shadow of death,

I will fear no evil;

For You *are* with me;

Your rod and Your staff, they comfort me.

5 You prepare a table before me in the presence of my enemies;

You anoint my head with oil;

My cup runs over.

6 Surely goodness and mercy shall follow me

All the days of my life;

And I will dwell in the house of the LORD

Forever.

CHRISTMAS

C	=	Christ (Keep Christ in Christmas)
H	=	Hope (Hope for a better life)
R	=	Resurrection (He Rose on the Third Day)
I	=	Idol (Christians do not Worship Idols)
S	=	Salvation, Savior
T	=	Truth (Jesus is the Truth)
M	=	Memories, Mourning for loved ones
A	=	Acceptance of Christ, Angels
S	=	Sacrifice

That's What Christmas Means to Us!

CHRISTMAS MEANS MORE THAN GIFTS AND A TREE

Pray for Our Government

Pray for our government, even when you do not understand. Mother and Fathers hold on to God's hand, for only He knows the true and perfect plan!

God Bless Our Troops!

Romans 13:1

God gives authority to those in government.

Pray for Our Government

Pray for our government, even when you do not understand.
Pray for our government because they are in authority,
And our lives are in their hands.

Pray for our government

So our love ones can soon all come home,
Never forget God has the ultimate plan.
For our country and none of us are alone.

Pray for our government for that is the key,
Key for our peace of mind and for our safety.

Mothers and fathers hold onto God's hand,
For only He knows the true and perfect plan.
God bless you troops!! We Love you and thank you!

Romans 13:1
God gives authority to those in government.

Suicide is Not the Way Out!

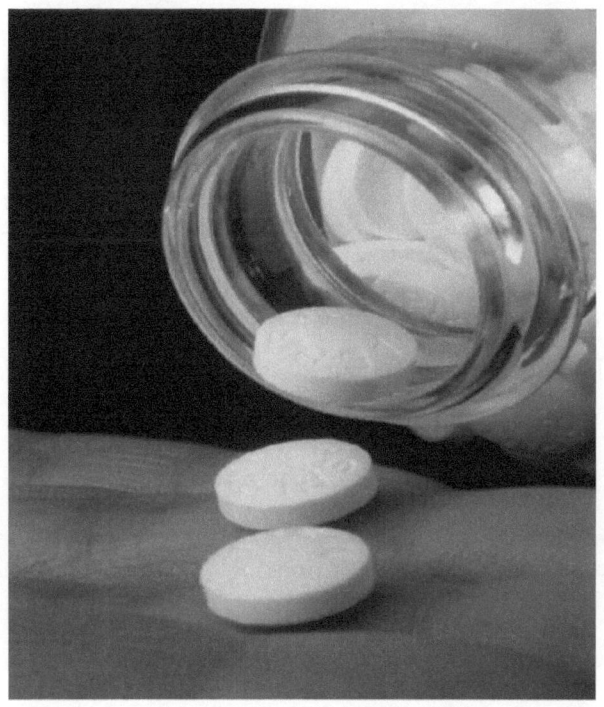

You want to give up because life is hard; your problems seem big. I know how you feel but SUICIDE is not the answer. Jesus is the answer and He is the way out.

JESUS CAN HELP YOU!

Suicide is Not the Way Out

Anyone who needs to hear this today,
Please listen to me, SUICIDE is not the way.

Many people have thought of this at some time in their lives,
Thinking SUICIDE is the way out!

You want to give up because life is hard; your problems seem big…
I know how you feel but SUICIDE is not the answer
Jesus is the answer and He is the way out,
Jesus can help you

Find a church, hospital, or personal friend you can talk to
Just know that Jesus is there for you
Through the hurt, suffering and pain

Let God come in,
Open your heart and open your Bible, too
Remember God loves you and He will comfort you
Again, SUICIDE is not the way out!

Parents, children suffering with mental illness,
Or who need a pediatrician that cares.

Contact: The Bethesda Clinic INC.
(Glorifying God through Spirit, Soul & Body)
1148 Pulaski Highway Suite 107-317
Bear, DE 19701, telephone number 302-266-0591
E-mail: info@thebethesdaclinic.com

Why Do I Celebrate Easter

The most beautiful thing I ever saw was in my imagination, when I saw your Son on the Cross. To thank you for His testimonies, His prophecies, His miracles and His suffering.

Matthew 27:63

Saying, Sir, we remember that that deceiver said, while he was yet alive, after three days I will rise again.

Why Do I Celebrate Easter

God I dedicate this to you! To thank you Father for your Son Jesus Christ to thank you for sending Him down on earth to show us how to live, to love, and to learn about you, to thank you for His testimonies, His prophecies, His miracles and His suffering. I am so grateful for your Son Jesus and that He died for our sins and rose again.

God, now I'm talking to you. Religion is so very controversial which to me is so sad, and to be truthful, it breaks my heart. I just want everyone to live with you. No matter how they get there. Just get there, and if that means accepting the most precious gift that you gave to this world your beloved Son Jesus, I pray that everyone does.

I also believe there will be all types of people, of different faiths praising your name and kneeling at your feet with you in Heaven. A new heaven, more beautiful than anything that We have ever seen thus far.

The most beautiful thing I ever saw was in my imagination, when I saw your Son on the Cross. Thank you again, I'll see you Father and your precious Son after my work here is done! These are the last days, so Soon it just may be time to meet your Son. your daughter, your child, humbly, Anelda L. Ballard P.S. your daughter Jean A. Scott loves you with her whole heart. I am sure that she is an angel just sent here on earth by you. As a part of your perfect plan. Thank you for my mother, I have been honored to be her daughter, and to be raised by a woman who is a living example of you and your Son.

Matthew 27:63

Saying, Sir, we remember that that deceiver said, while he was yet alive, after three days I will rise again.

DO YOU BELIEVE?

Do you believe that Jesus Christ died on the cross and rose again? Do you believe that the only way to be saved is through Jesus Christ the Son Of God because He is your Savior? Read John 3:16 and Romans 10:9-10 in any version of the Holy Bible If you do not understand it, READ IT AGAIN! The bottom line is DO YOU BELIEVE?

I want to give you and Invitation to be SAVED: Pray with a sincere heart: God, I accept Jesus Christ as my Savior, I ask you to come into my life, I repent for all my sins and believe that Jesus Christ is Lord and I believe He rose from the dead on the third day with all power in His hands. I want to serve you with my whole heart from this day forward. I will try to live the best Christian life, and put you first in everything I do. In Jesus' name I pray. Amen.

Or pray or own sincere prayer. Now, Read the Scriptures below:
(If you have done this you are now SAVED)

John 3:16

For God so loved the world He gave his only begotten Son, so whom ever believes in Him shall not perish but have eternal life.

Romans 10:9-10

For if you confess with your mouth that Jesus Christ is Lord and believe in your heart that God raised him from the dead, you shall be saved. For it is by believing in your heart that you are made right with God, and it is by confessing with your mouth that you are saved.

May God add a blessing to the reading of the word, Amen!

WHERE ARE YOU GOING?

Give you life to Jesus Christ Today!
AND GET SAVED

Call me Toll Free 1-877-782-5550 and talk to ME!

I MINISTER TO SOULS FOR THE KINGDOM!

Anelda Ballard "JAZZY KITTY"

Closing Prayer

Heavenly Father,

We say thank you once again.

Now that this assignment from you has come to an end.

I, your servant, pray from my heart

That this book will bless lives,

The way it has blessed my mother and I from the start.

Heavenly Father, in addition,

I am also asking for a special blessing for everyone in the world,

Especially for all the people that are hurting in any way.

Most importantly, Father…

I pray that the world accepts your precious Son Jesus Christ,

Who is my mother's and my Personal Savior.

Lord, if this book touches just one soul or life,

Then our purpose is done.

Heavenly Father, I want everyone to feel the same love for you;

And for your Son and prayerfully have the same relationship as we do.

In Jesus' name I pray. Amen (Touch and Agree)

Ephesians 6:18

Pray all the time.

POETRY IS OUR MINISTRY

**ASSIGNMENT COMPLETED,
TO GOD BE THE GLORY!**

www.ingramcontent.com/pod-product-compliance
Lightning Source LLC
Chambersburg PA
CBHW031300290426
44109CB00012B/666